Cultivating Your

Catholic Community

Helping Young Couples and Families

Find a Place in Your Parish

Monica Kimutis

To my husband, Jared. Thank you for your love and support! You inspire me to love more deeply.

To all family and friends. Thank you for your friendship and for being a part of my life! Without you I would have nothing to write about.

For bulk orders or group rates, please email jmjfamilyministry@gmail.com.

ISBN-13: 978-1548234164
ISBN-10:1548234168

Stay in the Know of Future Resources!

Read this first

There are many ideas that I want to implement for cultivating Catholic community in the future. If you want to know of future happenings or resources, please contact me at jmjfamilyministry@gmail.com!

I'd love to hear from you!

CONTENTS

1. "Family! Become what you are!" 11

2. Spiritual Goal of Ministry 29

3. Social Goal of Ministry 41

4. Educational Goal of Ministry 51

5. Groundwork 57

6. Obstacles to Family Ministry and How to
   Overcome Them..67

7. Parish-Wide Programs 77

8. Small Groups...81

9. Advertising and Recruiting...........................95

10. True Stories..105

11. What Can ONE Family Do? 113

12. Resources...117

INTRODUCTION

*"Encourage one another, agree with one another, live in
peace, and the God of love and peace will be with you."*
-2 Corinthians 13:11b

God desires our happiness. As a young, married
mother, I experience immense hope and joy in my
Catholic faith, and want to share that hope and joy
with others. While I am so grateful for the gift of
my vocation as wife and mother, *family life is hard!*

My husband, Jared, and I experienced and
continue to experience the need for a stronger faith-
based support network for families in the Catholic
Church. Jared and I moved to Tennessee soon after
we graduated from Franciscan University in
Steubenville, OH. Jared had landed his dream job
teaching theology in a Catholic high school. This
move brought us quite a distance from my family in
Idaho and from his family in St. Louis. It was a fun
adventure as newlyweds.

When we had our first child, we began to feel
more acutely the absence of our family. We needed
guidance with what to do with a newborn! We
needed help raising our son. Our second son came

soon afterwards. We desired close relationships that family bonds usually have with them. We wanted our sons to have grandparents nearby to build relationships. We wanted help with babysitting so Jared and I could invest more easily in our marriage relationship! We wanted aunts and uncles close by when Jared or I needed a night out. We wanted our sons to have strong relationships with other young children much like cousins might have if they see each other frequently. When holidays rolled around and we were unable to travel, we often felt left out or forgotten when our friends would be busy with their own extended family. We knew we were not the only young family missing out on these strong relationships because of a job located far from family. We learned from our loneliness that we would need to be intentional about building up relationships with friends who needed deep friendships as well. From our own loneliness and need, we recognized the same needs in many of our peers that we met through our church. We now dedicate much of our time to building up our Catholic community by bringing together young couples and families.

Jared and I experienced so much rapid change in our early twenties that we could hardly escape survival mode. But, we desperately wanted to belong to a church family and we needed Christian friends. Those things take time. A ministry can close that time gap and nurture its members, just like it has done for us.

I wrote this book to accomplish two goals. First, I hope to encourage newly married couples and young families along their journey of growing in their relationships with God. Christian life includes times of suffering and hardship. I desire to bring Christ's healing power to families today to spark in them the hope and joy that come from living out the Catholic faith.

Second, Christian families need support. In these pages, I illustrate how a family ministry can be built that will bring joy, friendship, support, and strength to your church community by supporting young couples and young families.

Families have a foundational role in our Church and can be a powerful means of bringing God's grace to those around them. In this book, I talk about the importance of a ministry to newlyweds and young families in the church. I then lay out the groundwork one must do to start a successful family ministry, for both parish-wide programs and small groups. I share ideas on how to create events and how to use advertising and recruitment methods to fill events with participants. I share obstacles you may encounter and practical solutions for overcoming them.

Last, I share success stories from our ministry's families. *It takes only one family to start a ministry.* I pray you find encouragement and support in my words.

Building community is a huge need in our Church. May God reward your efforts as you seek to serve others!

CHAPTER 1
"FAMILY! BECOME WHAT YOU ARE!"

St John Paul the Great encouraged families to fully embrace the role they were created to fill, saying, "Family, become what you are." What *are* families? They are powerful witnesses to God's love as they interact with the world. Jared and I must work hard to keep our marriage healthy. I rely heavily on God's grace to get us through difficult times in our marriage. When it feels like I have run out of ideas and energy, I ask God to take over. When I invite Him to work in my life, God responds generously. This type of work often calls for humility and openness. When our marriage thrives, we can give more energy to our children and others in our community.

LIVING IN COMMUNION

Each person is made in God's image. "God himself is an eternal exchange of love, Father, Son and Holy Spirit, and he has destined us to share in that exchange" (Catechism of the Catholic Church, Paragraph 221). In *Familiaris Consortio*, Pope St John Paul explains that because God is a communion of persons in the Trinity, a person is more in God's

11

image when living in a family than living as individuals. It is part of our nature as humans to be in community. Living in community is what we are made for!

Since we have a tendency to be selfish, it's often hard to break our habits of putting ourselves before others and God, and yet we must put God and others before ourselves to live in community. Love leads to communion. Sin leads to division. To live life fully in communion with others and with God, we need grace! Grace is God's life in us. We need God's grace to overcome sin. As Catholics, God continually offers us grace through prayer and the Sacraments of the Church. These are real instruments through which God gives us His life and the tools we need to live daily in love. The Sacraments of Baptism, Confirmation, Reconciliation, Marriage and the Eucharist are all conduits of this life-giving love that God wants to give us.

How the Young First Experience God in the Communion of Family

The human family reflects the communion of love that God *is* in His very nature. The Trinity is a Divine Communion of Persons. It is a community of life and an eternal self-giving love. Each person is called to participate in the life of the Trinity and reflect this love in their own families. One could consider the family to be something like a "mini-trinity", or a reflection of the Trinity, because the family is also a community of life and love[1]. When family life is lived well, the family reflects the Divine self-giving love of the Trinity to others.

The Holy Spirit is the shared love of God the Father and God the Son. In a family, the child is the shared love of the husband and the wife. Right away, when a couple has a child, a life of community is experienced in the family.

God works and speaks to us through others. My family teaches me about God. As my family grows in relationship with God, we can show the world who He is by how we work with and speak to others. My hope is that my family's words and actions reflect God's love for all people.

Children comprehend God through their parents. He is our Heavenly Father. Our Earthly parents set the first example of the relationship between a child and God. Children learn from all experiences, whether good or bad. Children ask questions. Is God faithful? Does He love me? Is God always available? Does He understand me? The way parents show their children unconditional love, mercy, gentleness and attention directly translate to their children's ability to experience a living God.

The Christian life requires a consistent habit of seeking an active, positive relationship with God.

---

[1] John, Paul II. *On the Family: Apostolic Exhortation, Familiaris Consortio.*

13

There are many similarities between God's action towards us and the model parents can provide to their children. God demands effort on our part. Parents demand effort from their children. God disciplines us. Parents discipline their children. God wants us to be spiritually mature. Parents should model maturity. God is also patient- fortunately much more patient than we are! God is patient with us as He invites us to love Him and to respond to His grace. God gives us the space we need to grow. If we stray from Him, He always welcomes us back. Parents have many opportunities to practice these merciful characteristics of God. Parents draw strength by leaning on God's grace to help them be holy witnesses to their children. Children, and adults, need a "cloud of witnesses" (Hebrews 12).

The Family is a School of Love

The family is a school of love. The Church is the family of God. We are children of God by adoption through baptism[2]. God's love for us is what makes us worthy of being his children. As adopted children, we grow in the womb of Holy Mother Church. In the Church, we should be supported and nourished by a faith community that helps us navigate life on Earth as we prepare for life in heaven. Just like an infant cannot comprehend what

---

[2] Catholic Church. Catechism of the Catholic Church paragraph 1997. 2nd ed. Vatican: Libreria Editrice Vaticana, 2012. Print.

life outside the womb must be like, humans cannot understand what life will be like in heaven. We need reassurance from the Church community. Our goal is to be united with Christ in Heaven, where He will fill our cups to overflowing with his Grace and love.

Both our human family and the family of the Church are needed for growth and support. My own faith is supported by others who share their faith with me. We can't make it to heaven alone. While it is true that Jesus is the one mediator between God and man (1 Tim 2:5), Jesus also invites us to be co-mediators with him. We are co-mediators with Jesus when we cooperate with him to bring others to heaven. Jesus commands us to "Go, therefore, and make disciples of all nations" (Matthew 28:19). Who will we bring with us to heaven? If you are married, your job is to lead your spouse and children to heaven.

A Christian's Communion with God

We begin our Christian life through the Sacrament of Baptism. God gives us the gift of His life through Baptism where we are adopted into His family as His children. As adopted children, we are given what is needed to live the life of Heaven.

Through the Sacrament of Confirmation, a Christian receives a greater outpouring of the Holy Spirit. The gifts a Christian receives all aid in fostering communion.

The Sacrament of Reconciliation restores grace to our soul after we have lost grace by choosing to sin. When I sin, I choose to reject God's will by selfishly choosing what I believe will satisfy me. Each time I sin, I come up short on grace. What seems appealing at first loses its taste. Sinful choices always disappoint eventually. Going to confession on a frequent basis has been a huge gift for me and my marriage with Jared as it brings me once again into the life of Christ, which is communion with Him. When I cling to God's grace, I remain in communion with God which is shown by the communion I live with others.

Living Communion by Way of Marriage

The Sacrament of Marriage is a reflection of Christ's love for the Church and God's faithful love for His people. Our primary example of God's love comes from Christ on the Cross! That is love. True love is willing the good of the beloved[3]. Willing the good of someone means that you desire for them what is in their best interest. Ephesians 5 encourages, "Husbands, love your wives, even as Christ loved the church and handed himself over for her". Loving someone in this capacity is selfless. Truly loving another person requires sacrifice and a willingness to take on suffering and pain for their benefit.

---

[3] Aquinas, *Summa Theologica* 1.20.3.

In marriage, a couple lives in communion with each other and with God. A couple's wedding vows of communion are renewed when they join in sexual union. The sexual act is a very real way that God bestows grace on the couple to fully live out their marriage. Again, grace means God's life in us. From marriage, grace spills over to the rest of the family. It is important, then, that a couple remain open to God working in their marriage by allowing Him to bestow grace when the couple renews their covenant through the marital act of sexual union. Therefore, the Church teaches against contraception. When a couple uses contraception, they interfere with the way God has designed their bodies and their marriage. Contraception cuts a couple off from the grace God wants to bestow on them.

The Church asks a couple to remain open to God's life and plan for their marriage by not using contraception. The Church understands that couples can find themselves in situations where postponing another pregnancy is the most loving thing that can be done. There are certainly many circumstances that are just reasons to postpone a child. The Church gives the couple space to determine what God is asking of them. The use of Natural Family Planning (NFP) to postpone children still allows a couple to love as God loves- by loving each other freely, totally, faithfully, fruitfully and permanently.

Natural Family Planning is often easy to learn but difficult to live out in marriage, especially when couples have grown up in a culture that promotes instant gratification and indulgence in pleasure. When a community supports a couple to keep pushing through difficult times in their marriage by not resorting to contraception, a couple is encouraged to live more fully in God's grace. Practicing NFP is not easy! Having others to talk to that know the struggle can be very helpful and healing.

Our culture promotes contraception as a "right". Even when couples are strong in their faith, they often lack resources and support to remain committed to church teaching regarding contraception. When couples have a working knowledge of NFP and not just a basic understanding, they are empowered to live out the beauty of the Church's teaching by avoiding contraception. I encourage all couples to gain a working knowledge of NFP. This includes couples who are engaged, married, wanting to have many children right away, or seemingly infertile. Even couples who are past child-bearing years can play a big role in encouraging younger couples to persevere in trusting in God's goodness by not resorting to contraception.

Living Communion by Way of the Family

A family's task is to reflect the life of the Trinity. When a family's home is a place of deep prayer, the family is strengthened to live a life that reflects Trinitarian communion. Frequenting the Sacraments is another way families are strengthened to live in communion with each other.

The role of parenthood springs forth from marriage. Spiritual motherhood and fatherhood can be present in every marriage even if the couple is not able to have their own biological children. Through my role of motherhood, I am given many opportunities to live out my Christian life by truly loving my children. Showing love takes on many different forms. Some forms of love can be quite painful for me especially if my children need attention in the middle of the night. Motherhood has called me to a level of love I had not experienced until now. There are sacrifices I make for the benefit of my children, whether that means forgoing physical comforts in pregnancy or choosing to spend more time with my children instead of other leisurely activities I also enjoy.

Now that I am a mother of small children, my prayer looks differently than it did when I was single. I cherish the memories I have of starting my days praying quiet holy hours before or after a prayerful Mass. While it still is needed for both me and my husband to seek out quiet time in front of our Lord in the Eucharist, we don't have the flexibility to go as often as we'd like. Communion with God is our highest priority, so we place a strong emphasis on prayer each day.

We have fallen in love with a merciful God and we want to help our children develop a relationship with a God who loves them more than we do. While the priority for prayer is high in our family, we are not always able to incorporate the ideas I'm about to share. Life with young children changes daily and we do the best we can while making sure our family's needs are met!

Rosary

Jared and I each consecrated ourselves and our relationship to Jesus through Mary at the beginning of our dating days. In this, we committed to praying a daily rosary. With some creativity and perseverance, it is a rare day that we don't pray a rosary- we love it so much! We recognize we need God's grace and don't like to let days go by without seeking His strength, His wisdom, and His power. Our expectations for how a rosary would be prayed in our family had to change as we had children and as those children became loud, noisy boys. For a long time, we prayed the rosary as a family as we walked around the neighborhood when the boys were still young enough to sit in a double stroller. Because of our commitment to pray a rosary, and because we found this to be the best way to pray this devotion, we went on walks every day. We have been surprised by all the benefits we have acquired from this routine.

We came to know many of our neighbors on our nightly outings. Our neighborhood became much friendlier in our eyes as we met more of our neighbors and learned their names. One particularly intriguing story is how we met Sha Sha, a grandmother who was visiting from China for a year to help her son's family as they transitioned to life after a new baby. Sha Sha did not speak more than 5 words of English, but she would take her older grandson on a walk each day. When she saw us, she would join us on our walks and teach us Chinese words. We ended up meeting her son's family as a result. We enjoyed the opportunity to share our love of the Rosary with her, and to encourage her and her son's family in their faith of Jesus. Sha Sha has since returned home to China. Before she left, she let us know we are always welcome in her home! We still enjoy our relationship with her son and his family who live a couple roads over.

Now that our boys are 4 ½ and 3, sitting in a stroller is not something we can convince them to do. They'd much rather be walking and hitting stuff with sticks. Our family rosary has transitioned to the boys' room in the evening as they calm down for sleep. Praying a rosary in this way still allows us to ask the boys what their intentions are, for what they are grateful, and for whom they'd like to pray.

Works of Mercy

Another way to pray as a family is by performing the works of mercy together. As a family, we will visit an elderly neighbor that was recently admitted to a nursing home. Volunteering with Meals on Wheels is another way that children can be involved. Children can also help make and deliver a meal to someone you know who is sick, or to a family who recently had a baby. Providing a meal to someone who is going through a tough transition is a way to show Christ's love. We are the hands and feet of Christ. By loving and serving others, we make Christ more present in our world.

Liturgy of the Hours

Liturgical prayer is the official prayer of the Church. Praying the liturgy of the hours as a family is a way a family can extend the prayer of the Mass to other hours of the day. The Church places a high merit on this prayer that has been given to us. An abbreviated form of liturgy of the hours may be necessary when including children.

LIVING COMMUNION WITH OTHER FAMILIES

"Where two or three are gathered in my name, there I am in the midst of them"- Matthew 18:20

The Christian life is not meant to be lived alone. Communal prayer has a powerful effectiveness and strengthens a community. By praying as a

22

community, we are stepping outside of ourselves and praying for others. Ways of living communion within a single family can also be used to live in communion with other families. By praying with other families, either at parish events or events held in homes, we show our children that praying is normal Catholic behavior! Prayer is central to developing a relationship with Christ. Children need to be shown how to pray. When children see other families praying alongside their own, children witness the strength of a community of faith and are supported in their own journey to a personal relationship with Christ.

Mass

We believe that offering Mass is the best possible thing someone can do in a day. We make it a high priority to pray the Mass as a family as much as possible. Sometimes we pray the Mass just once or twice a week, some weeks we are able to attend daily. Because of Jared's flexibility with his job, he is often able to join us for daily Mass. Other times, I take the boys solo. By going to Mass so frequently, the boys learn appropriate behavior during Mass and I can more comfortably take them by myself.

Don't get me wrong, we still have days where we feel like we weren't even at Mass at all due to how much we had to wrestle our children. Even if the family is in a season of life where the children aren't able to sit through Mass, having the parents attend

Mass on behalf of the family is still important. Offering up your prayers and sacrifices in union with the Mass is so powerful. Jared and I recognize the great gift that daily Mass is to our family and yet there are still times when we aren't able to go because of random events, or the boys (or mom!) just need a day at home.

Adoration of the Blessed Sacrament
One of my favorite ways to pray as a family is Adoration. Having my children in the REAL presence of Christ is healing for this mother's heart. I frequently encounter my weaknesses in this vocation of motherhood, and I'm able to offer to God my attempts. He is the one who can win my children over to a relationship with Him. I do what I can to help them get there.

Quiet adoration is currently only offered once a month at our parish. To help my children learn the value of Adoration, we organize family adoration hours. We schedule these events at the parish. Family adoration hours are complete with music and a prayer leader that help the children learn how to pray in adoration. The prayer leader is a religious sister, priest, or other parent who can lead the children in prayer. These are evenings filled with songs and silence where confession is simultaneously available by a priest. Fellowship with other families follows these holy hours. When families come to attentively listen for God's voice in

Adoration, Christ makes Himself known in powerful ways!

THE FAMILY AND THE CHURCH

St John Paul the Great taught, "As the family goes, so goes the nation and so goes the whole world in which we live." Imagine a society that is made entirely out of strong families. Families interact with the world. Living life as a *Christian* family means that we engage in our society and culture while keeping our sights and desires on heaven. Each family is a building block of society. Families have a profound opportunity to transform our culture and strengthen it. If families fully engaged this opportunity, then the peace of God would enter society through families.

Families who live their Christian faith well stand out from the secular crowd. Christian priorities are different. Virtues like simplicity and generosity do not scare you when you trust Christ to take care of your needs. As we exercise intellect and free will, we can draw strength from knowing we are not alone. We have the gift of supernatural grace to carry us through.

Christian families, even by just going about their daily business, intrigue those who witness them. If lived well, a Christian family's life can lead to the conversion of others who may have never had the opportunity to experience the profound love that can be shown in a family.

Jared and I have such a heart and a drive to serve families. We want to encourage families to discover the beautiful truths that await them. I admit: Jared and I go a little overboard sometimes and the needs of our family begin to take a back seat. We have also observed other fervent Christians who, in the name of zealousness for the Church, neglect their own families. The results are counterproductive to the couples' goals. Perhaps the marriage suffers, or the children lack attention they need at crucial moments. Jared and I try to be cognizant of this and make sure we take frequent breaks from ministry to ensure our own marriage and family's needs are being met.

Priorities

Jared and I married in 2011. In six years, we have moved away from family and friends, started two new jobs, had two babies (with a third coming soon), bought our first house (a mere 14 hours after the first baby came!), started living on one income, completed a Master's degree, and completed home repair and renovation projects. I'd say we are still in a whirlwind! What really helped was keeping our priorities straight. In her book *Mother's Rule of Life*, Holly Pierlot describes the "5 P's" of priorities. Jared and I take her words to heart, and by doing so, have found it easier to manage life, marriage, and parenting demands while still ministering to others.

Holly Pierlot recommends prioritizing responsibilities in the following order:

1. Prayer - Seeking relationship with God
2. Person - Making sure we are spiritually, physically, and emotionally healthy as individuals
3. Partner - Keeping the marriage relationship strong
4. Parent - Meeting the needs of our children
5. Provider - Providing for the financial and material needs of the family

Holly states that women consistently put their parenting role (#4) first, while men put their providing role (#5) before everything else. God must come first. Of course, emergencies will jumble priorities. Whether in or out of the routine, if nothing else, Jared and I know that our relationship with God is our priority. Jared and I each rely on God to fulfill our needs instead of expecting each other to fulfill that role. That makes everything else simpler to manage.

When, after the birth of our second child, life became overwhelming, Jared and I feared we would have to let the family ministry go. One evening, we sat down and listed every single one of our responsibilities. We then went through and numbered our responsibilities into the"5 P's" of priorities. We thought we'd see that we should take a break from building family ministry. We were shocked when that was not the case! Building community and empowering other young families around us fit in to our #1 category: Prayer and our relationship with God. Ministering to other families and building community is so important to our own family and our own individual needs that we can't let it go.

So, how does a busy family like mine build a community to serve others? We focus on three goals of family ministry: We examine how we can help meet families' needs of Spiritual, Social, and Educational growth.

CHAPTER 2
SPIRITUAL GOAL OF MINISTRY

*"I have given them the glory you gave me, so that they may be one,
as we are one, I in them and you in me, that they may be brought
to perfection as one, that the world may know that you sent me,
and that you loved them even as you loved me." John 17:22-23*

The spiritual goal of family ministry is to teach families how to daily connect closely with Christ in their parishes and homes. The goal is for Christ to be better known and better loved! To this end, a focus is placed on creating spaces and events where people will be more comfortable and relaxed to allow God to work more freely in their lives. Once families come to relaxed and comfortable environments with open hearts and minds, God does the rest.

I have a few experiences of being struck by the beauty of a space of prayer that really helped me enter into a deeper communion with God. Creating beautiful sacred spaces is not my forte, unfortunately! This is where it's so helpful to have a team of people working together, each bringing forth their own gifts.

Beautiful sacred spaces should not be distracting. Families will be bringing their children and children are distracting enough! All should point to Christ.

At the Parish
God sustains our life by holding us in existence. We can encounter God *spiritually* everywhere. As Catholics, we believe that Our Lord and Savior, Jesus Christ, is truly *physically* present in the Eucharist. Therefore, meeting in the parish is appropriate for spiritual events like Adoration and Mass.

APPROPRIATE SPACES FOR YOUNG CHILDREN
We want to encourage young families to participate in the life of their parish and greater faith community. Providing a sacred space where people are comfortable is crucial to helping people enter into prayer with Christ. You may have to exercise creativity to turn a room typically used for a different purpose into one that is safe for children. A larger room is more helpful when children will need to be entertained for a longer period!

Staffed Nurseries
Childproof rooms with age appropriate toys set aside for childcare might be a luxury for most parishes today. Our parish in Tennessee has been blessed with a new nursery. The nursery is so

popular that it is hard to find a day in the month that it is not being used by one group or another! Having the nursery consistently staffed by employees who are VIRTUS-trained eases the concern for meeting VIRTUS requirements. VIRTUS is a training program to ensure that the safety of children is upheld when adults are working among minors. Having several people who are looking for extra income by providing childcare and who are VIRTUS-trained is very helpful to ensuring young children are adequately taken care of for the time when their parents are engaged in faith formation activities.

Retreats

Strong families depend on strong marriages. An emphasis needs to be placed on supporting Catholic marriages to keep them healthy. It can be difficult for new mothers and fathers to both go on a marriage retreat together. One option is to make a day or one-night retreat for the wives and/or mothers and another one for the husbands and/or fathers. Each role has a specific calling, a specific vocation that needs to be supported and built up. Nurturing each spouse's relationship with Christ can ultimately strengthen the marriage and graces will then overflow to the family.

Another way to support the spouses is by providing times of spiritual development during family retreats. When putting on a family retreat, the main goal is to keep the family together as much as possible! We want to help the family encounter Christ *together*. With that being said, there are times when it is appropriate to separate the parents and children to engage with each demographic in a way that is best for them. Offering activities that are age appropriate for preschool and school age children will engage the smallest retreatants. Engaging the children in interesting activities is especially important for times when the family is separated for faith formation.

Having safe spaces for young children during retreats is necessary for families to feel comfortable. The needs of families with young crawlers or young walkers are often overlooked. Smaller, child-proof, carpeted rooms are most ideal in this case.

Retreats provide a much-needed break from the stressors of daily life. On retreats, families can reconnect with each other and with Christ. Times of group prayer during a retreat can include a family rosary, where each child holds a rose to present to a statue of Our Lady after each Hail Mary. Another idea is to have each child release a balloon that symbolizes the prayers reaching to the heavens.

I had the idea of putting on a family retreat for a few years before I worked up the courage and felt like I had enough support to organize one! If you are just beginning, a good option is to join larger organizations that host family retreats, many of which occur during the summer. You can help coordinate several families to take a road-trip to places such as churches, shrines or other places of pilgrimage. Another idea is to go to a place like Catholic Familyland and participate in their retreats together.

Quarterly or Monthly Events

Having consistent events for families at the parish is a great way to start building a family ministry. Offering different types of spiritual events will intrigue families who are at different levels in their spiritual life. One month, the parish can host an afternoon or evening for families to pray together in Adoration. The following month, they gather for a fun activity like a movie night. The third month, the families gather for an activity and time of prayer based on the current liturgical season.

To align with the spiritual goal of bringing families closer to the Sacraments, hosting quarterly Adoration nights is a great idea! Ideally, Adoration nights would be offered more frequently, but offering them quarterly is a good place to start. This is a space where young children are welcome to attend and even gather very closely to the Blessed Sacrament while their families are nearby.

Christ wants to heal families. Families are encouraged to encounter Christ physically present in the Eucharist when times of Adoration are geared towards welcoming their young children. Children are noisy and young families often find it difficult to bring their children to Adoration which is usually offered in an environment of silence. While I am a big advocate for including silence in one's day, I know that encountering Christ in the Eucharist can be a very healing experience. I want to encourage young families to draw on the grace available to them when they go to Adoration. This is done by having times set aside where the expectation will be a time of Adoration with more noise. It is very helpful to have prayerful music playing to help mask the natural noise of the children.

Musicians who are trained in praise and worship will be helpful in assisting participants to enter more fully into prayer. A worship leader who is comfortable working with young children and leading them in prayer can be a gift to his or her community. It helps for the worship leader to know songs that use body movements and hand gestures to help the children with those wiggles!

If a priest or deacon is unavailable, families can substitute Adoration by praying vespers in front of the Blessed Sacrament in the Tabernacle, or engage in songs of Praise and Worship. I have had great experiences where this has been well done at Franciscan University of Steubenville. Once families are familiar with the idea, then those who feel called can follow pastoral guidelines and complete special training to be on prayer teams to pray over people in a special way. When a heart is open to God, God can work in amazing ways!

Bible Studies

Homes of young families (even though they are often quite small) can be a great resource to provide space where people can grow spiritually in small groups. We talk more about Bible Studies as part of small groups in Chapter 8. I will mention here that parishes that offer Bible Studies at the church building can greatly enhance the experience of participants by encouraging the social aspect of ministry to take shape. When people develop stronger bonds with each other, they can dive more deeply into discussions and really wrestle with the truths of the Catholic faith to make them their own.

One-time Bible Studies can take shape in the form of a group *Lectio Divina*. When a group meets together for *Lectio Divina*, they spend time in silence with a passage of scripture. This could be ten to fifteen minutes. Then, people come together in a group to discuss how God spoke to them through that passage. I am often blown away by the difference in what people can take away from a few lines in the Bible! It truly is a Living Word where Christ is encountered. When we encourage and teach people how to listen to the voice of God, we can help strengthen their prayer life and relationship with God. This, in turn, strengthens the family.

AT THE HOME

The family is a Domestic Church, meaning that they live out the life of the Church in their homes. Family ministry has the goal of providing tools to families so they can better reflect the Life of Christ in their homes and relationships.

Having a sacred space in the home is also a great reminder to the family of their communion with Christ who resides in their midst. Our house is 1400 square feet in size, much like many other American homes. We converted a space into a little chapel. We keep that room set apart, and use it for prayer. My routine is to go in there as soon as the boys fall asleep at naptime. There I quietly drink deep of the living Water of Christ. It gives me great peace to have that small place where I can escape the pressing demands of life and allow Christ to renew my strength.

Catholics have a great gift in the Liturgical life of the Church. There are ways that the family can recall the Liturgy of the Eucharist and extend it to their homes. Living liturgically can be a fun way to engage children in the story and life of Christ. There are many blogs and ideas on how this can be done- from special meals, to decorations in the house, to activities or special prayers. My husband enjoys trying to match his outfits to the liturgical colors of the day. When he's teaching at school, his students know if it is a martyr's feast day, a doctor of the Church or Solemnity... just from the color of

Jared's tie. He initiated "Socks for Solemnities" at his high school, where students celebrate Solemnities by wearing fun socks as part of their high school uniform.

When a family fosters communion in their own home, a desire develops for communion with other families. Often, families are motivated to open their homes to share with others the beauty of their faith. Some families prefer meeting in each other's homes rather than at the parish. Sometimes, homes are more comfortable places for families with young children, or for families in which one of the spouses is not Catholic. Meeting in each others' homes can be a bridge to bringing families closer to the Sacraments at the parish in the long-run.

Childproof Homes

Small groups thrive when meeting in homes of their members. Having a childproof home creates a relaxing environment for young families to enjoy fellowship and better enter prayer or faith discussions. A home will ideally have a separate space for children to play. If the children are very young, a babysitter is recommended for events that focus on adult faith formation. Young families tend to live in small apartments or small homes that make this difficult. A fenced-in backyard can be helpful in the warmer months.

If a babysitter is volunteering or being paid while parents are engaged in faith formation at a home, they will need to be VIRTUS trained. Here is a sample of expectations that can be laid out up-front for members of a small group that are not VIRTUS trained:

"The JMJ (Jesus, Mary, and Joseph) Family small groups will include opportunities for faith formation that are inclusive of the whole family. On many occasions, the faith formation opportunities will be directed primarily towards the adults and onsite childcare will be provided by volunteers. To provide a safe environment for all attending the faith formation events, all adults present will be encouraged to attend local VIRTUS training programs. Furthermore, any adult who has not completed VIRTUS training will not be permitted to be isolated with minors present at the faith formation events. A VIRTUS trained adult must accompany any adult who has not completed training when they are in the presence of minors."

PARKS

Parks with enclosed areas for young children can also be a solution. These may be hard to find. If there is enough room on parish grounds, perhaps a small area can be made into a play space for young families to meet without worrying about their young children darting out into the road or parking lots.

FREE BABYSITTING

Young families are often still establishing financial security. Little funds may be available for a young family to consistently attend parish events if they must pay for babysitting each time. To encourage frequent participation, it is recommended to offer free childcare. If funds are not available from the parish, a family can pay babysitters and consider it as part of a tithe to the Church community.

High school students who are looking for service hours are also a great resource for babysitting for small groups. Having a list compiled of those willing to babysit for events or small group meetings can eliminate last minute stresses if a babysitter cancels

CHAPTER 3
SOCIAL GOAL OF MINISTRY

"Loneliness and the feeling of being unwanted is the most terrible poverty."- Mother Teresa

My husband and I know the sting of loneliness. Especially in big parishes, people can feel lost. Surrounded by so many people, I've often found it strange that I can feel so lonely. I desire to be known and to know others. I desire to have deep relationships with people that care about me and my well-being, and I want to reciprocate that care. When we moved about 2,000 miles away from family and friends to start two new jobs in Tennessee, I had a hard time making new friends. I was frustrated. I was lonely. I missed being a Christian friend. Jared and I especially feel this isolation when we are sick! Without family nearby, we felt the need for community in a stronger way.

We became parishioners at the largest parish in our diocese with 2,500 families. So many people were associated with the parish, yet we knew very few. Once we became more involved in our Church, there were summers we would leave for nearly two months to visit family in Idaho and no-one would notice our absence. I often thought, "If we were to disappear off the face of the planet, would anyone in my parish notice?" It seemed like the answer was, "No."

Because Jared and I both desired having close, family-type relationships even though we were away from the places where we grew up, we didn't want to give up on our fellow parishioners. We decided to *be* the change we wanted to see in the people in our parish. We wanted our fellow parishioners to be more welcoming and inviting. So we became more welcoming and inviting. We wanted parishioners to reach out to us, so we started reaching out to other parishioners. Jared and I ended up meeting a few other young adults who also expressed interest in getting to know other parishioners.

What started out as four people getting together for a time of prayer and then going out to a restaurant afterwards, turned into a group who met for consistent weekly meetings. After a couple of years, the scope of this little young adult ministry reached about 60 participants and it became officially recognized by the diocese. Now, five years later, over 220 people have been involved at some point!

We transitioned out of the young adult demographic once we started a family. Even though our friendships look a little different now, Jared and I still have taken the approach of introducing ourselves to other young families and coming up with ways that we can build relationships with them.

Organizing regular social activities helps families get to know each other and be open to including more people. As Matthew Kelly encourages, "care-free timelessness" is a necessity in building relationships. It's not a luxury. Families need good friendships. Having social elements included with all types of family ministry events encourages families to get to know each other better. When we know the families we are praying with, we deepen our sense of community and can better experience Christ in prayer with others.

When the parish supports social activities, the parish benefits by having members connected to each other. Families who feel known and cared for are more likely to attend Mass, participate in and contribute to parish-wide events.

You may want to design social events that respect the differences between young adults, young married adults, and young families. While there are many differences in these demographics, it is important to keep these people connected with each other as they all have gifts that can be used to build each other up. Ladies' Nights, Men's Outings and Couples' Nights are all great ways to bridge the gap between these different groups.

Ladies' Nights

What does any woman like to do for fun? The possibilities are endless here. Some ideas we've seen include the following:

- Wine and cheese nights at a parishioner's home
- Dinner out at a restaurant
- Clothing swaps
- Cooking meals for other families in need of extra support
- Book clubs - edifying Catholic literature can certainly enhance one's faith
- Crafting
- Cookie exchange
- Spa Nights at a parishioner's home

I love to see women work together to help other families. For example, a group might use the parish kitchen to make meals for families who have a new baby, are ill, or are grieving. They might do short mission projects for a poor school, like back-to-school supply drives, tutoring, or gardening services. If families have older children, they can be included when appropriate. What better way is there to teach children about having a servant's heart than by having the children serve side-by-side with their families and friends?

Men's Outings

I realize I am stereotyping here- but for the sake of finding examples, I've listed ideas for men to have fellowship while building their Catholic faith:

- Watching sporting events
- Playing sports (Think of the old-time church league softball games)
- Enjoying beer and wings
- Trivia night
- Camping
- Fishing
- Playing music together
- Service projects for the poor like building bunk beds or wheel chair ramps, painting or home repairs.
- Volunteering together. Imagine the powerful witness a group of men can provide by simply taking their children somewhere to do service work.

Couples

Social events can also promote healthy marriages. Support the spouses! Marriages are strengthened and renewed when couples spend time together away from the demands of their children.

It can be difficult for couples with young children to get out on their own. Couples with children can have a tough time finding reliable babysitters. Hiring babysitters frequently is often a financial burden. Couple time is crucial. There are solutions that alleviate stress and provide adult time for parents to relax and reconnect, which will strengthen the marriage and the family.

Keep in mind that young couples without kids are often more comfortable in environments where they can relate just as couples.

Examples of couples' activities may include:

- Quarterly or bi-monthly date nights offered by the parish. These can be done early in the evening with free babysitting provided.
- Couples may agree to a "sitter swap" in which families take turns sitting the other families' children so all couples have multiple opportunities per year to enjoy alone time or fun with a group of adults.
- For one semester, the couples involved in our small group made a commitment to paying for babysitters so we could get together at a restaurant without kids. We had some discussion prompts to help keep conversation mostly centered on topics of faith, but the emphasis was to keep a casual environment for couples to get to know each other. We really enjoyed these meals!
- One successful event we planned was a Valentine's party for couples practicing

NFP in their marriage. We were able to rent a clubhouse in our friend's neighborhood. It was a relaxing evening of games and good food! One couple oversaw party games while another couple put together prizes to encourage others to participate.

Families

Family fun activities are so important for strengthening the bonds and setting examples of Christian parenting and friendship. Family activities give children fun opportunities to be engaged with their parents. I've listed a few events we've tried:

- Families take turns hosting themed parties.
    - We've had a "pie contest" party where each family brings a sweet or savory pie as a potluck.
    - Lasagna and Lawn Games has been another fun social event.
    - A Three Kings Party complete with themed food and a traditional house blessing.
- We've also had fun at a parish "Hoe-Down" with a Barbeque themed dinner and square dancing.
- When the weather is nice, cook-outs at a park or in a host family's backyard is an easy go-to event. Families can share the meal potluck-style. Another easy way is for one

family to plan a main dish and have other families contribute side dishes, drinks, desserts, or money.

- Families can attend city-sponsored events together. Attending a festival with a group of other families is easier to organize. Children love parades.
- Family fun runs sponsored by non-profits can be an enjoyable experience.
- We live close to the Great Smoky Mountains National Park. Day hikes are fantastic ways to build community and experience God in nature.
- Any of the activities for men and women can easily be adapted to include children.

When we visited St. John Cathedral in Boise, Idaho, the church hosted monthly block parties during the summer months. After the Saturday evening Mass, parishioners gathered next to the church, enjoyed dinner from food trucks and live music played by a local Catholic artist. The church welcomed discussion with curious passersby and offered tours of the cathedral.

Providing some social events that are not centered around food can be a more welcoming atmosphere for those who have serious food allergy concerns.

On a side note, I'd like to encourage those with food allergy concerns to not let food keep them from participating in social events. Sometimes my family has a well-balanced meal before going to an event. It saddens me to hear of families who miss opportunities due to food concerns. The goal is to socialize with other families.

CHAPTER 4
EDUCATIONAL GOAL OF MINISTRY

"Each truth that we learn about God is a new reason for loving Him." -Frank Sheed

We designed our family ministry to build up participants' personal knowledge of the Catholic faith. As Catholics, we have an incredibly rich history. The Catholic Church's knowledge of faith and morals are the fruit of over 2,000 years of contemplation. We benefit from countless examples from the lives of the saints who teach us how to apply the Good News of Jesus to our daily lives through their words and examples.

The treasures of our Church are inexhaustible. We can strengthen our peers' faith by introducing them to the beauty of the Catholic faith. We can use many tools to awaken a sense of awe in others.

Opportunities for family education may include:

- Group Bible studies
- Video series
- Vacation Bible School

- Book Studies
- Inviting speakers who are experts on certain academic topics
- Seminars
- Panel Discussions

Because some aspects of our faith are academic, it's important to incorporate opportunities for small group discussions as a part of educational events. By sharing intimate thoughts about Catholic teachings, we encourage head knowledge to become heart knowledge. Small group discussions help individuals integrate what they've learned into their daily lives.

Questions such as, "What stood out to you or surprised you on this topic?", "What's your main take-away?", "What questions remain?", and "How does this apply to your daily life?" will prompt discussion. These discussions help people internalize the intellectual content they were exposed to during the educational event.

Again, while the goal is to educate others, we want to ultimately lead people to a personal relationship with Jesus and encourage them to experience the joy that comes from giving their lives completely to Him.

Allowing space and time for casual socialization can enhance the overall experience by helping people get to know each other and become comfortable with one another. When small group participants develop relationships, the small group discussions become more meaningful and better attended.

Providing childcare is important. Offering free childcare will increase the participation rate of young families. Families can participate in educational events in different ways. Some examples are:

- Families gather at a home where a guest speaker has been invited to present on a topic of interest for 30-60 minutes. A babysitter is paid to watch the children in a separate space to allow parents to focus on the topic at hand. Appetizers and desserts are served afterwards.

- Parents and children gather for a potluck dinner on a Saturday. After the meal, parents discuss a reading done in advance for about 30-45 minutes while very young children play at their feet. (This is a great format for a rosary if there are older children involved). After the discussion or time of prayer, dessert is served to encourage fellowship.

- Couples gather at the parish for a class while childcare is offered on-site.

TOPICS APPLICABLE TO NEWLY MARRIED COUPLES AND YOUNG FAMILIES

Below are popular topics of interest to young married couples and families. This list is just a starting point. The possibilities are endless!

- ❖ Natural Family Planning
- ❖ Communication Skills
- ❖ Finances
- ❖ Family Life as a School of Love
  - o Parents are the primary educators of their children. Teach parents how to educate their children in the faith.
  - o Parenting in a secular world
  - o The family's role in the Church
  - o Roles of Fathers/ Mothers
- ❖ Charisms
  - o A study talking about the existence of charisms in each person that has been baptized and confirmed.
  - o Discerning God-given gifts and how to use them to help others. The St Catherine of Siena Institute has phenomenal resources to help with this. Can you imagine a parish where each person knew what their God-given spiritual gifts were and exercised them?
- ❖ Church tradition
  - o Miracles
    - ▪ Eucharistic Miracles

- - Healings
  - Marian Apparitions
  - Lives of the Saints
    - Examples of married saints
    - Saints who were young adults
  - Ways to pray
    - The Rosary
    - Liturgy of the Hours
    - Stations of the Cross
    - Lectio Divina
    - Devotions
      - Novenas
      - Our Lady of Fatima
      - Divine Mercy
  - Types of Orders in the Church
    - Carmelite, Franciscan, Dominican, etc.
    - Lay orders
- ❖ Church History
  - Significant Events in the life of the Church
  - Early Church practices
  - The Protestant Reformation
  - The Crusades
- ❖ Apologetics
  - How to defend the faith
  - Introducing Catholicism to friends or family
- ❖ Writings of the Popes

- Couples can read letters from the popes ahead of time and meet for small group discussions to better understand the content.
- There are many great encyclicals throughout the ages. The popes' writings are meant for us as laity. Some to start with could be:
  - "On Human Suffering" by Pope St John Paul II
  - Pope St John Paul II's Letter to Families
  - *Spe Salve*
  - *Deus Caritas Est*
  - *Familiaris Consortio*
  - *Veritatis Splendor*
  - *Evangeli Vitae*

To pick topics, we survey the families already involved in our family ministry. What appeals to them at this time?

From time to time, we lean on high quality video series for group study. If you choose to use a video series, it is even more important to provide a time for discussions after the video. Also providing time for the participants to socialize will promote human connection in a culture that is already so digital and disconnected.

Chapter 5
Groundwork

"Patience and perseverance have a magical effect before which difficulties disappear and obstacles vanish."
- John Quincy Adams

ATTITUDES

Having the right attitude propels you past many situations that are not ideal. There are cultural atmospheres and facilities that will make a family ministry easier to start. With a "can do" attitude and persistence, Jared and I have come up with creative ideas and solutions that can be used to start a family ministry in your parish.

Humility

The work and sacrifice I put into ministry tends to make me proud of the fruits that God allows me to see. When things don't go my way or when I don't get answers that will make my life easier, I tend to get frustrated. I need a constant reminder that this work is NOT about ME. Any success I have at bringing people together so they may experience Christ in community is only a reflection of Christ's work in them. Family ministry is about making Christ known to our culture.

I get opportunities to practice humility when I approach complete strangers at Mass or other church events. Sometimes, I have great interactions with young families who are new to the area or are looking for a spiritual, social, and educational community of faith. Sometimes, though, I experience super *awkward* conversations with people who are obviously not interested in talking to me. My husband says my face turns bright red in embarrassment when this happens. Rejection is unpleasant. It is humbling. That is okay. I struggle to not take rejection personally. I refuse to let fear of rejection keep me from ministering to families.

To be practical, Jared and I set a simple goal: we try to meet one new family after Mass each week. We ask open-ended questions like, "How long have you been at this parish?", "Do you have family in town?", and "What brought you Tennessee?"

I may not make the most impressive or eloquent first impression. I often stumble on my words, but when I keep the love of Christ at the forefront of my mind, fear fades, and I am free to love as Christ loves. I am free to see others as Christ sees them. I am free to serve.

Perseverance
When I was in France as an exchange student my junior year of high school, I was really struck by a

phrase that was often used by the school community. "Impossible," was the response to many questions I posed. I never heard this word as an excuse when I was growing up. Always seeking to find a possible solution was the norm for my family when I was growing up.

Frustration can easily creep in if I don't experience consistent success. I think about perseverance, and try not to get frustrated when people don't respond the way I want them to respond. The devil wins when there is discouragement. If you are met with opposition or failure, don't give up. Try different events, ideas, and methods of reaching out to people. Persevere!

Respect

We often wondered why we cared so much about forming a family ministry when not many other leaders in our parish seemed as concerned. People serving on parish staffs have some big jobs and need our help to meet the needs of young families. Their distance from your efforts does not mean they are not supportive. They have many roles to fill. Maintaining respect and love for clergy and other parish staff will go a long way. Communicate with them often and openly. Your mutual respect will help as the family ministry grows.

Heart for Evangelism

When it comes to keeping the right attitude, fan your flame of desire for evangelizing! WHY are you spending so much time on ministry? WHO are you serving? Make Christ known! This work has little to do with you, and everything to do with glorifying God.

Consistency

People need to know what to expect with a ministry. Having consistent events decreases confusion for busy families who want to be involved in their Catholic community. Without a parish staff member focused on creating events, the parish may naturally have fewer gatherings. However, consistency *can* be achieved without a parish position. Someone must take the lead and bring community members together. Calendar consistency helps alleviate the leader's stress and promotes attendance. A team of people working on consistency helps out even better. One option to build consistency into the ministry is to start small with quarterly gatherings and build up to monthly events.

I have learned that planning three or four months in advance produces better events. Calendars and facilities are more often open for reservation; I have time to assemble a team; I am able to be more creative; I have time to build interest in the parish and follow up with invited guests.

Of course, young children can throw curve balls up until the last minute. Having a backup plan eases the tension. If you are not able to attend an event you planned because of sick children, the importance of team work comes in. Designate someone to run the event in your absence. Continuing events even when people cancel last minute will uphold the ministry's reputation for consistency.

Holding events even if you are expecting only one other family may lead you to wonder if it's worth the effort. We have had many powerful experiences when we continue the event as planned even when only one other couple of family told us they were coming. We've also had surprise attendees who end up benefitting greatly and becoming a very active part of the community! Continue the event as planned- even for just one. Rescheduling the event often discourages future commitment.

At the beginning of our family ministry, my husband and I were planning nearly every gathering. It became very draining and we were depleted of what we could give. We recognized the need to take breaks to re-assess our goals, needs and desires. We took breaks to improve our ministry efforts. Taking time off allows God to restfully restore your ambition and dreams.

Developing a family ministry is a big task. When one family spearheads the cause, there will be lots of room for improvement. Include others. Maintain consistency, but do not let your own family's needs fall to the wayside. Remember: the good spiritual health of your family plays a big role in transforming society. Lead by example.

COMMUNICATION

A family ministry exists to support families in their Christian vocation. Families need to know who they can turn to in support, so having an active, communicative network can be a literal life-saver. Consistency and communication work hand in hand.

Consistent communication can be as simple as monthly emails that provide brief updates on news and events in the community. The ministry's email list has been growing and I want to make sure the contact information of our group is protected. Be careful with members' information. I suggest using professional list software through secure websites like MailChimp or Flocknote. There are many free resources available for this. When people open their email, they tend to be in a position to make an action, so communicating via email can be a great way to distribute information and request members to participate.

Some ministries use websites, newsletters or group text programs. A steady presence on social media helps keep members engaged. A leader could easily delegate these tasks.

COMMITMENT

A healthy ministry will need committed people. Finding ways to motivate loyal participation can be challenging. When people don't feel important to a cause or community, they are much less likely to stay dedicated to the group. For this reason, we enthusiastically advocate for small groups for faith formation. Jared and I found that as our ministry grew in population and our events grew, we saw less passionate commitment from our members. We lost touch with some families and were not able to build our relationship as deeply with the addition of new families. We reassessed our goals and plans. We kept our goal to remain open and hospitable. At the same time, we wanted to protect the treasure that deep friendships truly are.

After taking a several-month break from active ministry, we invited four couples who would be willing to try a new format to join a small group with us. Our goal was to create a core group of families that would then go out and lead small groups of their own. This way, instead of having just one small group, we could potentially have five small groups.

Motivating people in a positive way makes a huge difference. It's easy to be "guilt-tripped" as Catholics. Personally, I am not motivated by wagging fingers and statements such as, "You *should* be more involved, give more, etc"

Think about ministry from a participant's point of view. Outside of Mass, why would anyone spend time with the Church community? The answer should somehow point to a love for Jesus. If families are not participating out of love, perhaps they have not personally experienced the merciful love of Christ in their own lives. Instead of judging in frustration, we must continue to invite and include. We must journey *with* our brothers and sisters and help them encounter Christ personally.

Remember that lack of participation may not always be a sign of lack of commitment. Young families have a lot going on. It often takes sincere effort for a family to get everyone out the door on time. Children are pros at throwing last minute tantrums and creating last minute messes. Empathy and understanding on the part of ministry leaders and group participants will create an encouraging environment.

Clear expectations and respect for families' commitments are necessary, especially in the context of small groups. It is helpful for leaders to be practical and reasonable. For example, it is easier for growing families to commit to smaller spans of time like a six-week Bible study, monthly outings, and quarterly dinners.

Respect for your own time is important, too. In the beginning, I didn't require an RSVP or registration for events. This put more stress on the planning side since I had no idea how many people would show up. I didn't want to deter anyone from coming at the last minute; I wanted to warmly welcome everyone. My concerns were unfounded. In my experience, it has been rare for people to show up last minute. They *want* and *need* to plan. Make it easier for everyone. Requiring an RSVP and registration makes it easier for everyone. Again, you can delegate this simple task.

MEETING COUPLES

The more Jared and I reach out to other young couples and families, the more we meet others who express a desire to find Christian friends. We have met many young couples and families through the NFP classes we teach. We also meet others who are interested in family ministry during church events and marriage preparation weekends.

My husband, Jared, and I have found that practicing Natural Family Planning has had beautiful and transforming affects on our marriage. We have experienced so many positive benefits from applying NFP in our marriage that we volunteer as certified teachers of Natural Family Planning with the Couple to Couple League. Through each class we teach, we meet couples who are taking their Catholic faith seriously. Most of our students express a desire for a community to support them while practicing NFP in their marriage and in their faith in general. NFP, while easy to learn, is hard to practice in a culture that values instant gratification. Christ shows us a different way. Even though a couple's decision to practice NFP is personal, we have found that we need a community of other couples who practice NFP to support us and keep us committed to Church teaching.

If your parish or church doesn't offer NFP classes, consider hosting preliminary informational sessions or becoming a certified NFP teacher. Connect with other NFP teachers in your area to learn how to support them in their NFP classes and create a collaborative relationship that will benefit your ministry and your parish.

Engaged Encounters or Marriage Preparation weekends are also a great place to meet couples. While engaged couples may not be ready to immediately commit involvement in their parish due to the stresses of planning for a wedding, you can follow up with them further into their marriages. Work with the teams who organize and host Engaged Encounters, Marriage Preparation, and other such events to learn how to identify and minister to young couples in your area.

Chapter 6

OBSTACLES TO FAMILY MINISTRY AND HOW TO OVERCOME THEM

"When we are sure that we are on the right road there is no need to plan our journey too far ahead. No need to burden ourselves with doubts and fears as to the obstacles that may bar our progress. We cannot take more than one step at a time." –Orison Swett Marden

Young families are overwhelmed. Young adults live in a time of intense instability and constant transition. Big life changes like a new marriage or new job are stressful. If young adults don't already have a strong faith and prayer life, they may feel it's too difficult to find the time to start one.

Young married couples conquer huge life changes in their first years of marriage. They tackle life's biggest stressors in short succession if not at the same time! They graduate and relocate to unfamiliar areas to start careers, often far from family. Many couples grapple with confusing fertility issues or NFP charts. Young couples birth children. Any parent will tell you a new baby does a great job at turning life upside down and shaking it around a little! Young couples buy their first homes and make many new first-time adult decisions. Young couples enjoy hobbies like playing or coaching sports. Mixed into all the new experiences of adult life, young couples navigate their religious identity and often negotiate religious commitments with spouses of different faiths.

Meet Families Where They Are

As leaders, we must understand and respect the changes young couples endure. Christ met the disciples on the Road to Emmaus. On the Road to Emmaus, the disciples were going the opposite direction they should have been traveling! Christ gently brought them back and allowed them to experience His love and presence. As we meet families where they are spiritually in our parishes, we want to show them Christ. Remaining free from judgment or negative emotions keeps the door open so that Christ may enter.

Just as Jesus met the disciples on the road to Emmaus, He meets us where *we* are. We must meet parish members where *they* are.

Most families in our parishes are not quite ready to prioritize their faith. Putting faith as the top priority only comes after the family has experienced the Love of Christ and has allowed Him to transform them by His mercy. If a parish is not actively evangelizing their parishioners, this could take a longer time. Conversion is often a slow process for families while they learn how to pray and nurture their faith. Through ministry, we can certainly provide opportunities for families to encounter Christ.

One of the perks for a family to have a strong community is for them to hear how other families live out their faith. How do other families pray with young children? If a family says they pray a rosary, it could look very different from one family to the next! One family might share how they only pray three Hail Mary's per decade, or how they wake up an extra half hour early in the morning so they can pray together before school. For a long time, we could only pray a family rosary if our two boys were buckled in a stroller and we went on a walk around our neighborhood. Maybe a family prays a rosary on their way to daily Mass. When families share what they have found to work, it can really encourage other young families who want to live a more authentic Catholic life, but may not know exactly how it can look.

Having mentor couples share their experiences raising their kids can also be valuable. Older couples have gained so much wisdom that can benefit younger families if it is passed down!

Sports and Extracurricular Activities
Our culture is crazy over sports! So many young children are involved in multiple sports at a young

age. Parents revolve their activities around practices and games. Families may not want to participate in consistent family gatherings if their free time is already full of sports commitments in the evenings.

Sports for children are not a bad thing! I benefitted in so many ways from participating in Cross Country from junior high through college. In high school and college, I grew in team leadership skills as a team captain. These experiences greatly enhanced my ability to be a team leader in family ministry.

I did not grow up in a strong Catholic community. It wasn't until my teen years that my family started putting faith first. Even still, it took a long time before we realized the priority that our faith community should have in our life as Catholics. Growing up, I believe our parish had great programs. It was the Life Teen Mass that really had an impact on my family's faith, especially my own. Sports and other extracurricular activities kept us away from community. In choosing sports over our faith community, we sure felt the absence of a strong support network.

Ultimately, we want to live life together with the other families in our parish community. There are so many ways we can do this and still meet families where they are spiritually. I remember hearing a story of how full-time FOCUS missionaries who work in parishes will meet families at their children's sporting events to engage in conversation there. It is beautiful to see families supporting other families.

Spouses of Different Faiths

It wasn't until I was 16 and going through Confirmation classes that my father started going through RCIA and entered the Catholic Church. Until then, my parents were not on the same page spiritually. For the most part, my father would support our family by attending Mass. However, the topics of faith and spirituality sometimes caused contention in my parents' relationship.

If both spouses are not Catholic, the couple may not feel comfortable attending explicitly Catholic events. Ideally, our family ministry is focused on supporting already strong Catholic families grow in a deeper relationship with Christ. But when it comes to ministering to families, there is an important element that Pope Francis accentuates. As Christians, our job is to go out to the "fringes" by serving and welcoming those who are at the beginning stages of discovering Christ. As families, we interface with the world and have many opportunities to go out to the fringes of our community!

Having a balance in the kinds of events offered to young families at the parish level can help non-Catholics become more comfortable with the parish community. The intention would be to lead them to a better comfort level with explicitly Catholic practices like Adoration of the Blessed Sacrament or recitation of a family Rosary. The end goal is to introduce these people to the beauty that these practices give to our faith. Being sensitive to meeting them where they are is a responsibility we have as Disciples. Love them. Serve them. Show them Christ in your actions and relationships so they, too, can experience God's Mercy through you!

Adult Hobbies

Every parent needs time and space for "self-care." This can look quite different for each person! My husband enjoys long-boarding around the neighborhood, watching a sports game or playing music. I'll sometimes go out with a friend, play music, take a nap or find a quiet spot on the river for some much-needed alone time. While we both schedule care time once a week, we keep our priorities in order. Our hobbies don't take a lot of time. However, some parents enjoy doing things that can take up a large chunk of time each week, require travel, or frequent babysitters. Sometimes the hobbies of parents prevent them from committing to consistently coming to family ministry events.

Holidays

We had a slow start to our fall semester of family ministry one year. We quickly learned that families focused on the holidays of Thanksgiving and

Christmas. The only hope of having family gatherings during these months is if you consistently have been meeting since August or September. The winter holidays with young children are exciting and young families are still learning how to navigate the seasons in our materialistic American culture. Trying to start consistent family events during the winter holidays will be difficult since families are often focused on preparing for Thanksgiving and Christmas.

Summer months tend to be slow and inconsistent for ministry, and most families will travel at some point. However, it could be that summer is a good time to focus on family ministry events that include the children, especially at outdoor spaces like parks or pavilions. We have found the best starting points to be the end of August/ first part of September or mid- to end of January.

Work Around These Obstacles

When you're trying to start a family ministry, it's easy to become frustrated if other families are not following suit or participating. Help families encounter Christ so that they are curious and hungry for the knowledge of the Faith. If a family knows the "why" of being involved in family ministry, they will not only be committed, but will become a strong force on your team.

My husband is a catechist and has a gift for teaching others the truths of the Catholic faith. Working with families, Jared and I notice some families are not ready to prioritize their faith. Often, this is due to either one or both spouses not being evangelized or catechized well before they became parents.

When a couple first gets married or has their first child, there tends to be a greater openness to change since they are already going through big life transitions. Both Jared and I notice that the first thing they desire is not to be taught the doctrines of the Catholic faith, but to be *evangelized*. Evangelizing is sharing the Good News of being saved from sin, of Christ and Salvation. Families need to experience the love that God has for them in this fundamental way. Catechizing is going into greater depth about various topics of the Catholic faith. Desire for knowledge of the Catholic faith will come naturally after evangelization has occurred.

Adult faith formation has the potential to be a huge game changer if it is done well in our parishes. Especially at the young adult level, we can start to form our young families before couples are even married. The organization called FOCUS (Fellowship of Catholic University Students) is having an impact at the college level. FOCUS sparks the desire in students on college campuses for a relationship with Christ. The organization starts forming disciples to spread the good news.

When young adults graduate, they need continued support as they develop habits on their own and as parish members. Young adult ministry serves young adults after college until they are married. Finding a way to link all these life stages can be beneficial to all involved. Each life stage has something to give to the other life stages. We are all in this together! For example, young adults can play the role of aunts or uncles to young families with children. Young families can help those who are not yet married see into the beauty and chaos of family life. When young adults are discerning their own vocations, having relationships with young families can help with this discernment.

CHAPTER 7
PARISH-WIDE PROGRAMS

"Whoever remains in me and I in him will bear much fruit, because without me you can do nothing." John 15:5

The parish keeps us connected to Christ. Through the graces of the Sacraments, we are given the strength to be faithful and fruitful disciples of Christ. The parish can be a hub of family activity. Because many parishes are large, the goals of parish-centered activities are different than the goals for small groups. With parish-based activities, the emphasis is on the health of the community.

Parish functions provide opportunities for newcomers to meet other families and become acclimated to the parish culture.

Our secular culture already separates the family too much! The family must grow together. With all events at the parish level, an emphasis needs to be placed on intentionally bringing people together, while supporting family units.

PARISH CULTURE

If a parish is not growing, it is dying! Parish atmospheres that are inviting will feel welcoming to new families.

What can pastors do to build community?

Pastor-led formation to guide a parish to become more open, merciful and welcoming to families can go a long way. Pastors can encourage parish events to be easier for young families to attend. An example is offering family events in late afternoons on weekends.

Pastors can encourage their families to participate in small groups. More detailed information on small groups follows in the next chapter. To keep small groups plugged into parish prerogatives and missions, the parish could encourage a strong emphasis on well-trained small group leaders. Leaders of small groups need guidance and support from their parish to ensure that their small group functions the best that it can. Having the small group leaders trained by pastoral staff is a great way to keep them from burning out. Small group leaders need support to work through issues that come up in facilitating small groups and working with their members.

Pastors can provide spiritual direction to families who are involved in building community in their parish. If you are a family that is jump-starting ministry in your parish, it can be very helpful to have a spiritual director that can guide you and encourage you. My husband and I have each met with our spiritual directors monthly for years. It has helped us work through tough times of discouragement, or when it has been difficult to know what to do next.

What can parishioners do?

Parishioners of different life stages can encourage each other in different ways. Parishioners without children can offer their free time to assisting young families participate more fully in the life of the parish. Parishioners can create events geared towards young couples and families, volunteer to set up or clean up these events, or watch the children during faith formation opportunities.

God put the wiggles and noises in children. Parishioners can create a family-friendly parish culture by showing mercy to young families at Mass. Parishioners can do this by showing an understanding attitude towards noisy children. Another welcoming gesture is for those without young children to let families sit on the outside of the pews. Families with young children often have to leave at some point during the Mass. Making it so that caretakers don't have to climb over as many people is often appreciated.

What can young parents do?

Young parents can make it a priority to attend events offered by the parish. If the way an event is set-up, or the time it is offered is hard for you to commit to because you have young children, you can clearly communicate your needs to help improve situations. Offering suggestions in a spirit of collaboration will go a long way.

Chapter 8
Small Groups

"But as it is, there are many parts, yet one body."
- 1 Corinthians 12:20

Jared and I advocate for small groups because we have found them to be the best solution for overcoming modern isolation in our parish. Deep friendships are encouraged in these groups. Participants are supported by the other members as they develop habits that catalyze their growth in faith.

Small groups differ from larger parish functions in that they provide a format where couples and families can personally wrestle through their struggles with a supportive, tight-knit community. The goals of these smaller communities are different from events held at the parish-level. In small groups, people can receive encouragement in the face of their own moral struggles pertaining to faith and culture. Ideally, each family will participate in a small group that is ultimately tied to the larger parish community. Imagine how transformative this could be to the Catholic culture if everyone participated in a supportive small group!

FORMING THE FAMILY

Small groups can be a great opportunity to form young Catholic families. Especially as young couples are wrestling with their new vocation(s), small groups can provide a solid foundation for families to learn what it means to be holy while living in the world. Striving for holiness in today's society is often dismissed because of people's false notion that holiness or sanctity is reserved for the priests and religious.

One of our pastoral associates, Fr. Pontian, tells a beautiful story of how small groups of families are the norm for the village in Northern Uganda in which he grew up. The whole village was one family. When a villager died, everyone attended the funeral. Everyone prayed. Everyone grieved the loss of a family member.

During the months of May and October, the local church divides the villages into small groups composed of a few families who meet regularly in each other's home. These groups meet weekly or daily. During their meetings, families share their stories with one another and discuss how to share God's story with the Sunday scriptures or lives of the saints. Small groups also recite the rosary and pray novenas together. In small groups, people help each other to make connections between everyday life and faith. They also reach out to their brothers and sisters in faith who are most in need.

These groups are not just about meeting an

individual's needs; they're also about building up a parish community and strengthening the life and mission of the church. Small groups really make a difference in the lives of those who participate in them.

Jared and I desire relationships with other Catholic families who have much more wisdom than we do. This was especially true as we were raising our first child who was not even a year old. We were constructing our own family identity, arranging our priorities and developing habits. We desired guidance from more experienced couples but had a hard time building relationships with couples in a different life stage. We were very fortunate to find friends that were going through our same stage of life that included new marriages, new babies, new jobs, new houses, etc. There is value in walking through all these transitions with peers and we learned a lot from them.

GOALS OF SMALL GROUPS

The following goals are adopted from FOCUS and helpful to keep in mind when working with small groups.

Deep Transformation

With God's grace, deep transformation occurs in small groups. When families encounter Christ, they fall in love with a God of mercy. This in turn leads to a deeper commitment to the Church that Christ established as they see the beauty in God's plan. Faith is deepened through faith formation studies. Also in small groups, participants are encouraged to share their faith with others. Small group participants are strengthened in their own faith by hearing how God has worked in the lives of their peers.

Communal prayer can have a powerful effect. Families are encouraged to pray together. Small groups can help open the door of faith to people who may be on the edge. Families not only pray for each other, but also for each other's intentions and in praise to God. When the small group invites the Holy Spirit into their midst, you can be sure God will not refuse! He rejoices in our openness to His life in us.

Deep transformation by way of a real relationship with Christ is encouraged in a small group. Small group meetings are fantastic environments in which to wrestle with the truths of the Catholic faith. In the small groups that Jared and I have been a part of, hot topic issues like same-sex attraction, modesty, and marriage issues emerge. Natural Family Planning also comes up quite a bit in discussions. Small groups provide an environment where people can discuss their questions openly, better understand Church teaching, and apply their faith more personally in their daily lives.

Intimate Fellowship

Life is all about relationships. This motto is one that my husband and I heard from Matthew Kelly. It has been one we've adopted over the past several years as we have discovered the value in intentionally building community. When friendships become more intimate, deeper struggles are shared and we are better able to walk beside our brothers and sisters on their journey towards Christ.

For intimate fellowship to occur in small groups, it needs to be an intentional goal. I have been a part of small groups that were focused on delivering content. Once the study had finished, most of the participants were still strangers to me, even though I had met with them and seen them nearly every week for 10 months! We want to promote growth in friendship. Friendship and intimate fellowship happens when we share life together.

Intentional conversation starters can be a big help when people are just getting to know each other. One of my favorite conversation starters is "highlights and lowlights." At the beginning of any small group meeting, each person in the group takes a turn sharing either a highlight or a lowlight, or a significant event that occurred since the last time the group came together. Sharing prayer intentions is another way to shed light on what a small group participant is going through.

Christ and His healing power can be made known in deep conversations or timely encouragements. We can let ourselves be channels of God's grace to others in our small group when we allow ourselves to be vulnerable with each other and let God work through us.

Spiritual Multiplication

The height of the Christian life is union with God. We are unified to God when we learn to love as God loves. As our love of God grows, so does our love of all people. As a Christian grows on his journey towards God, the Christian becomes a disciple. A disciple is someone who studies the ways of Christ and follows Him. Christian life doesn't stop there! Eventually, the fire of the love of God burns within the disciple so much he or she becomes an evangelist. An evangelist is someone who wants to share with others the joy that comes with discipleship. The evangelist shares this joy by spreading the good news about Jesus to others. An evangelist wants to help others become disciples themselves and ultimately, the evangelist becomes a disciple-maker.

The small group format can be a cocoon to help Christians become disciple-makers. For this to happen, small groups must be open to growth by welcoming new members. The current members of a small group benefit when they seek ways to invite others to join their group and to share their love of Christ more intentionally and intimately. Eventually, a small group reaches the point of spiritual maturity and then it is time for them to break out and spread the good news with other families. This can happen slowly. In our case, it happened rather quickly. To accommodate other families who wanted to be a part of the special bonds we were creating, we prematurely broke up our small group to branch out. This is where I learned about the small group life cycle. The steps here are important!!

LOGISTICS

Catholics can learn from our protestant brothers and sisters. Many of the non-denominational or protestant churches in our area far surpass us when it comes to building community through small groups. I met with Jesse at a local non-denominational church in my area. He pointed out practical ways Jared and I could improve our work with small groups.

Jesse introduced us to the idea of a small group life-cycle process. At first, the small group members need to develop a bond with each other so the members can become comfortable sharing life together. As the relationships are strengthened, members are then free to grow deeper in their relationship with God together. Eventually, small group members encourage and support each other so that their individual relationships with God prompt the members to want to invite others into the small group experience. This is an opportune time for the small group to break into two or three groups to welcome new members.

STARTING SMALL GROUPS

It is helpful for families to have a common experience so they can more easily relate to each other in a small group. This can be done in a couple of ways.

Topical Studies

Jesse suggested offering topical studies so families with similar interests could attend events and get to know each other. After the topical study finishes, families have the opportunity to continue meeting together in a small- group format. There are many great programs available that can be a starting point for small groups. A couple of examples are programs like ALPHA or Christ Renews His Parish. These programs incorporate group exploration of the Catholic faith. They consist of regular meetings in which small groups are formed. Parish support is needed for these small groups to continue meeting so they don't die out when the program is finished. The purpose of small groups is for families to share life together. When a program or topic finishes, it is important for the small group to continue meeting so that they can continue sharing life together.

Retreat

Evangelization retreats that are focused on family needs are another great way to offer a common experience to jump-start small groups. Encouraging families to intentionally build relationships during a retreat is an effective way for families to be less apprehensive about committing to small groups for the first time.

Group Size

We have found that an ideal size for a small group is four to six families. Any time a small group gets together, it's common for one or two families to miss the meeting. Illness, vacation travel, work, and family issues compete for time. Hosting four to six families for each event ensures that small group meetings take place even if several families can't come. Also, more than six families may create an environment where some feel they won't be missed if they don't attend.

Very quickly, our first small group grew to about 11 families which was way too many for one living room, especially when you consider all the children! For groups that become too large, Jesse stressed the importance of helping small groups keep the mindset of eventually going out to reach more families. One of the end-goals of a small group is for the members to break off into other small groups.

FREQUENCY OF MEETINGS
Once a Month

This approach seems to be the most comfortable place to start when first building a small group community. Meeting once a month is not intimidating especially if there is a short-term commitment. Busy families can often fit this into their calendar, especially if the monthly meetings take place on a weekend. These meetings can be casual or formal. Spiritual aspects as well as social can be incorporated into small group meetings.

The monthly meeting format is how we started building community once we had an infant. We had a handful of families meeting once a month. At the time, all our kids were very young- most were not even walking. This was great for a while, as it even allowed for discussion on topics like the Letter to Families that St. John Paul wrote in 1994. We also went over St. John Bosco's letter on discipline and the preparatory catechesis for the world meeting of families in Philadelphia in 2015.

Through our experience, we recognized a downside to monthly meetings. Monthly meetings were too infrequent to build solid relationships with other families. This was especially the case when kids became ill and families couldn't meet. We could go three or four months without interacting with a family who was in our small group if we had to miss a month, and then they had to miss the following.

To build solid relationships with families, we decided to try something radical. We wanted to try something that seemed unheard of in the Catholic sphere (but not to FOCUS!).

Weekly Meetings
A friend told us about an idea from FOCUS that could allow families to have some interaction with each other on a weekly basis without it being too overwhelming. A willingness to commit to weekly meetings was needed ahead of time from the small group members. We started by trying a weekly commitment for one semester. Our format looked like this:

- Families gathered for a spiritual or a social event once a month.
- The next week, the women gathered for a small group bible study. In an uplifting and faithful environment, we worked through how church teaching and our faith applied to our own everyday lives. This was a priceless gift. It takes courage to commit to a small group in this way, but it is so worth it!
- The following week, we gathered as couples.
- The fourth week in a month, the men met to go over the same bible study material their wives had worked through. I enjoyed hearing my husband's thoughts on what he

learned after he came home from those evenings.

The semester we tried this format was one that was filled with growth and encouragement for us. We made sacrifices that were painful so that we could keep our commitment to weekly meetings. The benefits we enjoyed still stick with us today as we grew closer to the families in this small group.

When we asked for feedback from the other families after our first semester of using this format, they also expressed how much they enjoyed this rotation. However, meeting each week added stress to their lives and most of them wanted to see meetings max out at three per month, with the couples meeting happening once a semester or quarter. For some families, paying a babysitter was expensive and they were only able to budget one babysitter a month. For the health of their marriage, couples needed to be spending more alone time with each other.

We had a clear end-time for this format which helped families commit to it in the first place. We took a break for a summer and then tried to expand the availability of small groups to other families in our community. Because most families didn't know each other, the thought of committing to three meetings a month was too intimidating. Most of the small groups who did meet regularly kept to the once a month plan initially.

HELPFUL CONSIDERATIONS
Dual Captains

From our experience, it is pretty taxing on our family to be the sole leaders of a small group. We learned to delegate or ask others to take ownership for the success of the small group. Having at least two families work together to lead a small group reduces stress and allows for consistency in coordination, communication, preparation, and completion.

Keep Families Connected to Parish Life

Ideally, Sunday Mass will feel like a weekly family reunion for those involved in small groups. Imagine how much more familiar and friendly a large parish would feel if families also journeyed through life together!

Extended Reach of the Pastor

In large parishes, our pastors and staff have a lot on their plate. Pressures placed on pastors can be reduced by healthy small groups. Instead of couples or families coming to the pastor for support, issues can often be remedied at the small group level as small group members take on the role of Simon and help their brothers and sisters carry their crosses. This ultimately can ease the burden on parish staff, since problems can be solved at the small group level.

When small groups effectively strengthen their members' faith, they strengthen their members' ties to the Church. Small group leaders can extend the reach of the pastor as they help the pastor in his role of spiritually leading the members of the community.

CHAPTER 9
ADVERTISING AND RECRUITING

"When you know your Why, you can endure any How"
- Viktor Frankl

Sometimes I get tired. Sometimes I feel like we've done enough. Most of the time, though, I'm restless. I want to see our family ministry grow; I cannot bear the idea of settling. My heart aches for young families in need. I am encouraged to continue reaching out to families as our ministry grows. New members energize and revitalize our community with their gifts, ideas, and perspectives. New members reward our efforts with zeal and gratitude.

Every Catholic is called to be a disciple of Jesus. Every disciple is called to evangelize. Jared and I have adopted this motto from Matthew Kelly: *Life is all about relationships*. We have found this motto to be helpful when discerning and prioritizing. Strengthening relationships assists in building up the Kingdom of God. When Jared and I consider which activities to participate in, we put a high priority on building relationships.

As much as building family ministry is a spiritual mission, I admit that it strikes similarities with the recruiting and sales processes. As a businesswoman at heart and by education, I apply marketing logic and tools to my efforts. I remind myself that it takes six "No's" to earn one "Yes". When families reject invitations, don't give up on them. Circumstances change. Their needs change. I remind myself that God constantly invites us into relationship with Him and we don't always readily respond.

Personal invitations are powerful. We have infinitely greater success by personally inviting people to our events as opposed to relying on bulletins and flyers. *Forming Intentional Disciples* by Sherry Weddell illustrates the plight of our parishes where a shocking number of people who enter our parish doors for the first time, are never greeted, and never return. This has motivated me to personally reach out to families I see at church. Sometimes families are brand new to our parish; sometimes the families have been long-time members and I just haven't met them. I have even been known to "meet" families more than once. I have to remind myself to be grateful when opportunities for humility present themselves in this way!

When we first meet a new family, we ask if they'd like to be kept informed of upcoming events. We ask for their email and if they use Facebook. Then, we follow-up with families we have met by reaching out to them through our email list and adding them to our local Facebook page of young, Catholic families.

Frequently reminding families of upcoming opportunities or events is another lesson I've learned from the business world. Families need enough time to plan ahead, then a few reminders on a consistent basis as the event approaches.

In my practice of meeting new families at church, I met Erin and Mark[4] whom I write more about in a later chapter. Erin is a crucial team player as we now work together to build family ministry in our diocese. Jared and I are routinely surprised at how many families we meet who have recently moved to East Tennessee. We've only lived here for 5 ½ years. In this time, we've built a network of families that is a benefit to other newcomers. Our memories of feeling isolated motivate us to work hard to see our community flourish.

ALLOW GOD TO LIVE THROUGH YOU

It is easy to spot a Christian who talks the talk but doesn't walk the walk. If you want to attract families to your family ministry, you must "walk the walk" and demonstrate Christian peace and joy. When it is in the family's best interest, this may entail daily Mass and frequent Adoration. Allow family members to rest in silence so they can better learn

---

[4] Names have been changed for privacy.

to hear the voice of God in their hearts. Frequent confession is powerful and healing. Communal prayer time as a family keeps the family connected to Christ. Praying together the Liturgy of the Hours (even an abridged version) or the Rosary are ways for the family to remain receptive to the grace God has for them. When praying together, a family can keep their daily lives united to Christ.

NORMALIZE IDEAL CATHOLIC BEHAVIOR

As more ideas and opinions are discussed, the more normal they seem. There are behaviors we would like to see every Catholic possess. Behaviors like evangelism, knowing Bible stories, attending frequent Bible studies, or participating in weekly small groups are behaviors often associated with Protestants that every Catholic could also benefit from. These are behaviors that could be normal for Catholics, too. Catholics begin to normalize certain behaviors by living them out in their own lives. Our habits and routines are spread by word of mouth in casual conversations, one-on-one, or group discussions. Jared and I have continued discussions on a larger scale by submitting articles in the diocesan newspaper and magazine.

What do we want our Catholic peers to show to the world? We want the world to see Catholics in happy, supportive fellowship with one another. We want the world to see Catholics live lives so virtuous that they intrigue others to ask about our faith. Imagine what we can teach the world through our witness of joy. We are Easter people, and Alleluia is our song!

BUILD A TEAM

Undertaking the task of starting a family ministry makes me feel a lot like the little boy with the five loaves and two fish in the Gospel of John, chapter 6. The weight of the need of all the people gathered to hear Jesus could have crushed the spirit of the boy. It could have been easy for him to succumb to embarrassment at the thought of even offering such a measly amount.

Begin with one small step. Next steps appear as you continue trying different things. A community can start with you. Ask God to give you guidance and bless your efforts. Ask God to bless you with help from others. Jared and I are one family with no extended relatives in town and with small children of our own. The weight of the needs in our community can be overwhelming. There is so much to do! We have built a team of other families that also recognize the need and can add their own small amounts of bread and fish to our distribution baskets.

The little boy who presented the five loaves and two fish to Jesus had a team to help him distribute. God's grace multiplies our initial offering.

Find Team Members

Sometimes, it takes a one-on-one invitation for someone to help with a particular aspect of ministry. Most families who have grown up without community and "gotten through it" may not even recognize the need to support up and coming young families in the area. Ask individuals again and again. Writing a letter to the parish through a newsletter or bulletin insert is a helpful way to let people know of the need.

Wanting to collaborate with our parish staff, we found we did not have any staff member specifically assigned to adult faith formation. We went to the diocesan level, and found our goals fell between two offices: Christian Formation and Marriage Preparation and Enrichment. Persistence led us to collaborate with both offices to find the support we needed to grow the ministry in our area. We happily heard, "Let us know how we can help." It took us a while to articulate our needs. Once we identified how the parish, pastors, and church *could* help, we worked with them to find solutions and opportunities for our ministry.

Ask to clarify what your parish or diocesan staff are willing to do to help you in this project of building family ministry. Articulating your needs might be difficult at first. Having them written down is a good way to communicate clearly.

Divide Tasks

Once you have several other families willing to help, you can delegate tasks that may include:

- Creating and sustaining an email list
- Designing a website
- Designing and printing flyers for events
- Distributing flyers to area parishes
- Creating ideas for events
- Hosting events
- Recruiting other volunteers and babysitters to help with specific events
- Managing social media like Facebook
- Building relationships with priests in the area and inviting them to events

Relying on other families' interests and skills is a great way to include others in the mission and allow them the opportunity to experience the joy that comes with providing meaningful service to the Church. At first, I tended to want to serve others and just do it all. I didn't stop to think that I was depriving others of being involved and feeling important to the success of the ministry!

USE PARISH RESOURCES

Even if family ministry is not a priority (yet!) in your parish, there are resources that most parishes will share.

- Consistent bulletin announcements will let others know you exist and what you offer.

- Place advertisements, events, and contact information on the parish website so young families can find you.

- Ask the pastor and deacons to announce events and encourage attendance.

- Post flyers where people gather: the narthex, the coffee station, childcare drop-off points, etc.

- Some parishes have social media accounts. Keep a consistent presence on the parish's social media and encourage people to comment and share links.

- Advertise in other parish groups. Our parish has active women's and children's ministries, as well as some men's groups, but others do not.

- We also welcome participants from other churches.

Know good times to approach people. Parishioners going through baptism and marriage preparation often have a wider range of openness to try new things as they transition to a new stage of life. Develop relationships with the people who oversee preparation for these sacraments. Those leaders may collaborate with you to recruit and serve new families.

National Organizations

Starting discussions with national organizations like the Knights of Columbus or the Council of Catholic Women can provide support and encouragement. The Knights of Columbus were founded to support the family, especially widows and children, and they still have that focus today. Perhaps the local councils would be interested in collaborating with you as you seek to support young families.

Partner with Catholic Schools

If you are looking for more interest in families to participate in your events, getting the word out at local Catholic schools could lead to a large response.

Most Importantly- Don't Give Up!

Success in a ministry is not about the number of people involved. We are successful in God's eyes when we are doing God's will. God works through us to help others come to know Him. Keep inviting families into community. Keep hosting events when you feel called to do so. Praise God when you grow more in love with Him through the events that also strengthen your family!

Chapter 10
True Stories

"Where one alone may be overcome, two together can resist. A three-ply cord is not easily broken."-Ecclesiastes 4:12

Building community in your parish has many benefits. These are just a few of the stories we have heard that illustrate some of the wide-ranging affects a family ministry can have on a community.

Miranda and Stephen[5]

Miranda and Stephen conceived their first child very soon after their wedding day. Overwhelmed by all the new demands of parenthood and life with a newborn, they resorted to using contraception for a while after their daughter was born. After some time, they could sense the strain that using contraception was putting on their marriage. They wanted to follow church teaching and knew that giving Natural Family Planning (NFP) another try was what they needed to do.

We met Miranda and Stephen soon after the birth of their first child at an introductory presentation for a Billings model NFP class. Jared

---

[5] Names have been changed for privacy.

and I had been recently certified as NFP teachers through the Couple to Couple League. We were interested in learning more about other NFP methods and to get to know others who were promoting NFP in our diocese.

Stephen and Miranda were also parishioners at our church so we often saw them on Sundays. Stephen and Miranda soon welcomed baby number two a bit sooner than they had originally hoped. Though they were grateful for a child, they were also a bit frustrated and confused with NFP; they knew there had to be more answers and support if they were going to keep practicing NFP. We enjoyed teaching them in one of our course series. Stephen and Miranda made valiant efforts as they navigated postpartum NFP while Miranda returned to work. Practicing NFP was still not an easy aspect of their marriage. It was not helpful that signs on charts were confusing and Miranda's return to work also included some travel.

Whether a couple practices NFP in their marriage is a very personal decision. Despite this, we have found that we all need a community of support to encourage couples to keep pushing through the tough aspects of NFP. Practicing NFP can be a life-changing practice and can strengthen a marriage if a couple persists. Having a family ministry that builds up marriages can transform our parish culture, and the culture in which we live.

Stephen relates,

Having the group was the best thing for me, particularly as I was struggling with the method. I did research online about how to adapt to the method and was discouraged by what I learned. Basically, couples were giving up because of how much it affected the husband. Talking about any issues and knowing that we all were going through the same struggles made things easier for me. For example, it helped just having the validation that the method was inconvenient or difficult for multiple reasons—like missed temps or variables outside our control that impacted the temperatures. It took lots of communication with Miranda for sure.

So, having the encouragement, despite how difficult or inconvenient the situation was, made a big difference for me.

Stephen and Miranda are now great assets to our family ministry. Even though both spouses are working full-time and they now have three young children ages six and under, they frequently open their home to host social events. When other couples struggle with practicing NFP, Stephen and Miranda are quick to listen and encourage them.

This family is also involved in parish life in other ways. Miranda supports Stephen by taking on more family responsibilities so Stephen can usher at Sunday Masses and volunteer his time teaching English as a second language and Financial Peace University at the parish.

ERIN AND MARK[6]

I met Erin and Mark after an Ash Wednesday Mass two years ago. It was one of those out-of-the-blue, awkward conversations where all I knew about them was that they had a baby. I approached them and introduced myself, "Hi! I see you have a baby. I do, too. My name's Monica…." I learned they had just moved to our area and desired to become more involved in the church community.

Erin and Mark moved from Atlanta where they enjoyed a vibrant young family community. They wanted something similar here in our parish.

Erin understood how the addition of a new baby shifts couple's priorities and interests. Young families find themselves on different schedules than their peers who are not married or don't have children. This makes social events difficult. Having an understanding church community is ideal. Erin asks, "What can be done better? What do families need?" To support the ministry, Erin manages our email list and sends out monthly letters on upcoming events. Erin and Mark also host social events. Erin experienced and values what family ministry offers, and is an invaluable support as she seeks to replicate what she enjoyed in Atlanta here in our diocese.

---

[6] Names have been changed for privacy.

JARED AND MONICA

Jared and I have each had excellent experiences with community. My experiences started in high school with an active Life Teen program at my home parish. Volunteers that led this program did a tremendous job at introducing me to a life of faith with Christ. Masses were engaging for me. The retreats that LifeTeen put on were effective at providing a space where I could personally encounter Christ in a very real way.

I attended Franciscan University of Steubenville. As a young woman, I relied heavily on others to model how to be a faithful Catholic. What did daily prayer look like? How did practicing faith as a college student look? I learned about redemptive suffering from my teammates while on the cross country team. My faith grew because I was a part of a dynamic community of Catholics.

Now, as young parents, Jared's and my faith lives are strengthened by other young parents living and demonstrating faith. I know I will not get to heaven alone. I need others. I will have others to thank when I get there through God's mercy. I want to bring others to heaven with me.

Life with Christ is much better than trying to make it on your own! Jared and I truly cherish this gift of faith we have been given, and want to share this way of life we know and love. It has transformed the way we live and love others. We are motivated to build community in our parish so our children can better participate in the life of the Church.

Jared and I also need mentors. With each life-changing event we've gone through starting with marriage, baby #1, baby #2 and soon-to-be baby #3, we desire to know the wisdom other families have gained. What kinds of habits or activities are appropriate for children? When do we know we are ready to welcome another child? When we consider career opportunities, we want to draw from insights of others.

Building community has been a great benefit to our family. Our family is strengthened through our relationships with other families. Jared and I are motivated to continue building community so that others can experience the many benefits of being more involved in their parish.

JARED'S VISION

Jared decided to study theology so he could teach at a Catholic high school. His vision was to help the high school students encounter Christ and develop a faith life so that they would be strengthened enough to keep practicing their faith once they went to college.

After six years of teaching, Jared realizes more and more that college students aren't falling away from their faith during college because they don't have a strong enough faith carrying over from high school. He has realized that his high school students rarely have a solid foundation in faith. To begin with, many don't go to Mass on Sundays with their parents. Six years of teaching has taught Jared that parents must model faith lives if they want their children to continue living out Catholic values. So, there is a great need for adult faith formation.

Jared has been motivated to offer adult faith formation opportunities knowing that it will only serve families in our community over time. Jared hopes to see strong families help their children develop their own faith before they get to high school.

CHAPTER 11
WHAT CAN ONE FAMILY DO?

"It's better to light one candle than to curse the darkness."
- motto of The Christophers

Just one person can have a large impact on his or her community. Let's start with just one. Let's start with YOU. Let's start with your family.

If you are feeling a need for a stronger community of families at your parish, start building that community you seek. Introduce yourself to one family after Mass. Look to see what the upcoming events are in your parish or diocese and invite that family to join you. If nothing appeals to you, invite them over for dinner one evening or perhaps a Sunday brunch. Keep a list of people you meet. Save their contact information. Make notes on how you met them. If you don't have a family ministry now, one could develop down the road. It will be easier to reach out to these people you have met if you take notes now.

Start building a team from your group of friends. Other families will see your excitement and express interest in growing deeper in their faith and being part of a close-knit community. Learn their interests and skills. Invite them to become active members

113

of a team so they can use their God-given gifts to enhance the ministry.

If you meet enough families interested in starting a small group or in meeting more frequently, it is important that you *remain open to newcomers*. Once you do have families involved in family ministry, following the suggestions in previous chapters will help ensure success. But, don't let imperfection slow you down. Allow God to work miracles in your life. It is important for families to meet. Even if the event is not perfect, families being together is better than not meeting at all.

TAKE THE NEXT STEPS!

Plan. Move forward. Seek guidance from a spiritual director in the church. Persevere! Give yourself time to learn, adjust, and improve. Give yourself time to rest. It's likely that you will have to keep a spirit of humility. The more time, energy and effort you put into building a family ministry, the easier it is to think the success is only due to your hard work. This is not about you- It's about glorifying God. It's about making Christ better known and better loved! With all of this, it's also helpful to remember the words of St Teresa of Calcutta: "God does not ask us to be successful, only faithful."

You will make personal sacrifices as you build a family ministry in your parish. Remember that no matter how much you give to God, He will always be much more generous. He loves you! He loves to give!

Keep your own family the top priority. The biggest witness and best way to build up our church is to fulfill your duties to your family first.

Most importantly, PRAY! Our Lady is a powerful intercessor as she, too, wants to make her Son known and loved by all.

It is my great joy to journey with you as you build a stronger support network in your parish. Please reach out to me to continue this conversation of how we make Christ better known and better loved by our families! I'd love to hear from you and your experiences. Please send me an email at jmjfamilyministry@gmail.com.

RESOURCES

The Couple to Couple League
Jared and I are certified teachers of the Couple to Couple League (CCL). CCL builds joyful marriages by teaching Natural Family Planning couple to couple. Classes are offered online or in-person: www.ccli.org

Fellowship of Catholic University Students
FOCUS wins the hearts of college students, builds them in the faith and sends them to the world: www.focus.org. Jared and I appreciate using their free bible study resources at: www.focusequip.org

Catherine of Siena Institute
The Catherine of Siena Institute works to make apostolic formation and support readily available to all lay Catholics. Jared and I have benefited a great amount from their Called and Gifted Workshop: www.siena.org

ALPHA
Alpha is a series of sessions exploring the Christian faith, typically run over eleven weeks: www.alphausa.org

Christ Renews His Parish
This parish spiritual renewal process was recently added to Dynamic Catholic's programs. A new website is coming soon. More information can be found at dynamiccatholic.com

THANK YOU FOR READING MY BOOK!

This project has been a big learning experience. I know I still have a lot to learn, and I would appreciate any feedback you have to improve the next version of this book and future resources.

Please leave a helpful review on Amazon to let me and other readers know what you thought about the book.

I look forward to hearing from you!

To Jesus through Mary,

Monica Kimutis